BRITAIN'S HERITAGE

Beach Huts

Karen Averby

AMBERLEY

Acknowledgements

Wholehearted thanks and appreciation are extended to the many individuals with whom I have communicated during the course of research for this book, both familiar and new. I am indebted to all who allowed their wonderful photographs of beach huts to be used to illustrate the text, and am extremely grateful to those who kindly provided cherished family photographs, stories and anecdotes; these could easily have formed another book in their own right.

County record offices have been invaluable resources for historical information and I would particularly like to thank staff at Hampshire Record Office, East Sussex Record Office (The Keep), Essex Record Office, Suffolk Record Office (Lowestoft), Somerset Record Office, Plymouth and West Devon Record Office, Durham Record Office, Dorset Record Office, Cumbria Record Office, and North Yorkshire Record Office, with special thanks to Tom Richardson of the latter for his valued advice and assistance.

Warm thanks are extended to my editor Nick Wright for his patience and encouragement, to Genevieve Bovee for keeping the home fires burning and to Luke Mouland for being my proxy at Dorset. Special heartfelt thanks are reserved for Patricia Pradey (my original inspiration), Michelle Doig and Jenny Guest for their unwavering support and encouragement from afar. Unreserved special thanks go of course to the amazing Jay Garrett for his indefatigable support, stoicism, patience and humour; my appreciation goes beyond words.

First published 2017

Amberley Publishing
The Hill, Stroud
Gloucestershire, GL5 4EP

www.amberley-books.com

Copyright © Karen Averby, 2017

The right of Karen Averby to be identified as the Author of this work has been asserted in accordance with the Copyrights, Designs and Patents Act 1988.

ISBN 978 1 4456 6574 0 (paperback)
ISBN 978 1 4456 6575 7 (ebook)

British Library Cataloguing in Publication Data.
A catalogue record for this book is available from the British Library.

Printed in the UK.

Contents

1 Introduction   4

2 Particulars   14

3 People   31

4 Places   43

5 Present   57

6 What Now?   62

1
Introduction

Britain's coastline is one of great physical diversity, with rugged cliffs, secluded sandy coves, vast open beaches, and a myriad of seaside towns and villages each with their own character. It is estimated that there are at least 20,000 beach huts located at these varied resorts, which have become integral to the landscapes they inhabit, nestling among sand dunes and cliffs, dotted along promenades, following the undulation of the shore line, standing in regimented rows at the beach head, or lying in random groups to form small beach hut villages. The traditional beach hut form of a simple, rectangular, wooden shed-like structure with a pitched roof is familiar everywhere, but there are many variations. There are terraced huts, huts on stilts, huts with porches and huts with platforms, as well as huts built of brick and concrete. They are a familiar visual landmark, and yet they emerged as a seaside fixture only relatively recently, at the dawn of the twentieth century – a development that was the culmination of a transformation of the coast that had begun two centuries or so earlier.

Before the eighteenth century the coast was very much the domain of fishermen and other sea-faring folk but, from the seventeenth century, there began a transformation that would change this status quo forever. A desire for improved health and a belief in the therapeutic and curative nature of the seaside, especially seawater, led to the development

A cheery group of brightly coloured traditional beach huts on the shoreline at Felixstowe, Suffolk. (Martin Pettitt)

A placid line of beach huts on the Isle of Wight, painted in shades of blue. These are a variant on the traditional beach hut form, and are divided into two rather than forming a single hut. (Carol Davis)

This Grade II listed brick-built terraced hut block in Cromer, Norfolk, was built in 1912 and is among the earliest and rarest surviving example of planned beach hut facilities. (Duncan Harris)

Above: This beach hut 'village' at Walton-on-the-Naze, Essex, is formed of lines of colourfully fronted traditional-style huts. (John Fielding)

Below: A line of cubesque huts at Thorpe Bay, Kent, are accessed via steps leading from the shore, set just above the high tide line. (Sue Chillingworth)

of the first coastal resorts. These were the preserve of the 'wealthy and idle', who visited them together with fashionable inland spa towns for recuperative purposes. The miraculous medicinal properties of seawater were believed to be far superior to the cures provided by the inland spas, and by the 1740s they were widely publicised by prominent physicians, notably by Dr Richard Russell, who went on to publish his ideas in his *Dissertation On The Use Of Sea Water In Diseases Of The Glands* in 1752. He prescribed regular drinking of sea water for every conceivable ailment, and immersion in the sea to strengthen and invigorate the body.

The burgeoning practice of sea bathing, already practised at Brighton in East Sussex and Scarborough in Yorkshire, increased in popularity as a result. Nude bathing for both sexes was initially commonplace; however, although men continued to bathe naked until the 1870s, it became increasingly common for women to wear bathing attire from the end of the eighteenth century, and it was thereafter pretty much expected. Mixed bathing was usual in the early days, but segregated bathing beaches were soon introduced, not only between genders but between social classes, and able bodied and disabled people, although this was difficult to police.

A perceived need for privacy while bathing led to the appearance of bathing machines at seaside resorts from c. 1750, often closely linked with bathing rooms where people drank seawater while waiting for a vacant bathing machine, as at Ramsgate in Kent and Hastings in Sussex, or at resorts where the number of bathing machines was too few, as was the case in 1750s Margate in Kent. At non-beach resorts, or at beaches where bathing machines were impractical, seawater baths were constructed, notably the Tunnel Beaches at Ilfracombe in North Devon and Plymouth Hoe in South Devon, which had a tidal pool by the mid-nineteenth century.

The bathing machine was primarily functional, and remained basically unchanged in appearance from their introduction in the 1730s until as late as the 1930s. Most were basic wooden carts, usually rectangular, fixed onto an undercarriage mounted on axles with two or four wooden wheels and a pitched pyramidal or curved wooden roof, some with bargeboards, and small sliding or louvred openings in the sides or roof for light and ventilation. Some might simply be a wooden frame covered by a canvas. The wheel size and width of the structures

Scarborough, North Yorkshire, 1735. Scarborough was one of the earliest seaside resorts and had developed from the 1720s, although it had been visited as a spa town since the seventeenth century. Engraving by J. Harris.

Left: A woman dives from her bathing machine head-first into the sea. Despite the modesty hood she can probably be seen from the shore. *Venus's Bathing (Margate)*, 1790, by Thomas Rowlandson. (Wellcome Library, London)

Below: Margate Quaker Benjamin Beale's 1753 design for a bathing machine had a modesty hood – a hinged and concertinaed canopy that could be lowered and raised to shield the bather from view. (Wellcome Library, London)

depended upon the type of beach and the depth of the incline. Crucially the bathing machine had to be both tall and wide enough to accommodate upright standing, and all sartorial challenges presented by large cumbersome crinolines and voluminous bathing shifts. Some machines were designed for more than one occupant, as at Weymouth, Ramsgate, and Gorleston-on-Sea. The machine was entered by a beach-facing door and would be hauled out to sea, often by horse but sometimes by manpower. The bather would then exit into the water via sea-facing steps.

The earliest machines were not overly successful in protecting modesty and a number of patents and designs followed that allowed the bather to enter the water hidden from view. The prospect of immersion in the sea alone was undoubtedly daunting as well as dangerous, especially as very few people could swim; swimming or floating in the sea was widely regarded as unnatural. It was therefore necessary to hire people to assist with bathing to prevent being swept away. Initially fishermen and their wives were employed, but over time the role evolved into 'bathers' for men and 'dippers' for women.

The popularity of the bathing machine was cemented by the use of a specially designed octagonal machine for George III at Weymouth in 1789, and it soon became a lucrative business as they rapidly became familiar sights at resorts all around the coast, often where there were vast beaches. At Aberystwyth in mid-Wales, sea bathing was current from the 1790s and, within a decade, there were four bathing machines for women and two for men, which had increased to a total of 126 machines by 1826.

Right: A gentle scene showing women bathing in the sea near their bathing machines. Engraving by J. Leech, nineteenth century. (Wellcome Library, London)
Below: The reality of sea bathing? This cartoon shows Brighton bathing machines at the shoreline – clearly not a pleasant experience for everyone. George Cruickshank, nineteenth century.

THE BATHING BEACH, BRIGHTON, IN 1846

The Bathing Beach, Brighton, 1846. As well as bathing machines and bathers, there are also people enjoying the beach, but fishermen's boats are still part of the beachscape. Lithograph by G. F. Bragg after a drawing by R. H. Nibbs.

Did you know?

Queen Victoria had a custom-built bathing machine, which she used at her private beach in Osborne Bay, Isle of Wight. Far more elaborate than pedestrian contraptions, it had a curtained verandah, a toilet, and was wheeled into the sea on stone tracks and winched back up afterwards.

The social exclusivity of the earliest seaside resorts changed from the early nineteenth century with the rise of the prosperous middle classes. Whereas the rich had tended to stay at their own houses built or purchased at seaside spa resorts, or as guests of friends and family, the middle classes stayed in hotels, and demand for accommodation and entertainment grew. Populist resorts emerged as improved and relatively cheap travel by rail or steamer from urban areas became available, as at Llandudno and Rhyl in north Wales, enabling the working classes to travel to places further afield within a relatively short space of time. The railway network opened up access to the coast and, as the rail network grew, so did the number of seaside towns, from early nineteenth-century resorts at Teignmouth and Torquay to early twentieth-century seaside towns including Cromer and Sheringham.

Very soon, obscure and even previously non-existent coastal villages were transformed into seaside resorts as entertainment and leisure become paramount and the seaside became

Bathing machines at Bognor, Sussex, with bathers in the sea, late nineteenth/early twentieth century. The number of adjacent rowing boats with families in and around them shows how the beach was being enjoyed by non-bathers.

available to all. As classic seaside entertainment fixtures appeared, among them funfairs, amusements and other such gaudy delights, the genteel character of many resorts disappeared.

Meanwhile, radically and rapidly changing social attitudes hugely impacted upon changes in the use of the beach. Increasingly liberal attitudes towards bathing had emerged by the end of the nineteenth century and bathing from the beach became more common, without the need to be first secreted within a box. Swimming was popularised as it gradually became an acceptable form of exercise, and both indoor and outdoor freshwater and seawater pools were built for swimming rather than for bathing. The bathing machine was soon regarded as old-fashioned and largely became redundant as private bathing for health gave way to communal, public use of the sea and beach for pleasure through swimming and sunbathing. Segregated beaches had never been popular and were in decline by c. 1900. At the same time changes in beachwear underwent a complete transformation as attitudes towards modest dress and behaviour on the beach relaxed.

The new forms of beach activity still required changing facilities, however, and these were provided in the form of beach tents that were hired out at seaside towns, often by enterprising individuals. Frequently brightly coloured and patterned, they were common fixtures up until the late 1930s. This period also saw the emergence of the beach hut as a more permanent structure for changing into and out of beachwear. Although bathing machines continued to be used by those who still required privacy, mainly by the older generation or more modest individuals, this was increasingly infrequent and by the 1930s most bathing machines 'were literally high and dry at the top of the beach'. Some were burnt in huge bonfires and others were advertised for sale in the local press, as they were repurposed for allotments, sheds and chicken houses. Many were de-wheeled and converted for use as beach huts.

The beach, Gorleston-on-Sea, Norfolk, 1920s. Bathing machines are still out in force, but there are also many bathing tents, with several huts among them. Within a few years these tents were wholly replaced with huts occupying the same positions.

A very crowded beach at Teignmouth, Devon, c. 1932. There are many people enjoying the sea, but bathing machines are not in use.

The nation's beaches were closed to the public during the Second World War, and beach tents did not reappear when beaches reopened in the late 1940s and 1950s. With bathing machines and beach tents dispensed with, thereafter the beach hut became the dominant and enduring beach structure, soon extending onto adjacent promenades.

Small Hope Beach, Shanklin, Isle of Wight, 1930s. The beach is crowded with people and beach tents, and there is a line of beach huts at the foot of the cliff.

Felixstowe, Norfolk, 1930s. Many rows of beach huts dominate the landscape.

2
Particulars

As the coast transformed from a functional working environment characterised by working ports and fishing villages to the place of leisure and enjoyment that we know today, so the beach hut came into being. Initially used primarily as changing huts, they soon became permanent spaces in which to linger and enjoy the beach in relative comfort.

Demand for such spaces was met in part by the widespread construction of municipal huts, as local authorities recognised their potential as lucrative sources of revenue, and from the early 1900s they grew to form a significant proportion of the nation's beach huts. Privately owned land at seafront locations was also used for the rental of beach huts, as at Hipkins Beach at Walton-on-the-Naze, Essex, from at least the 1930s, and very occasionally private estate land came onto the market specifically for the construction of beach huts, as at Southbourne, Dorset, in the 1920s, although such instances were rare. More common was the lease of council-owned land as beach hut sites for the construction of private huts; this was also a lucrative revenue source for councils, as not only were hut owners responsible for the maintenance of their huts, they were also liable for rent and rates.

At a basic level the form of the beach hut has visual similarities with the once-prevalent fishermen's huts and the bathing machines that were fixtures of Britain's beaches for

Brodick, Isle of Arran, early twentieth century. A common scene of people enjoying their beach huts at the beach. Brodick's popularity as a resort eventually declined due to a general reduction in seaside visitation and issues of beach erosion.

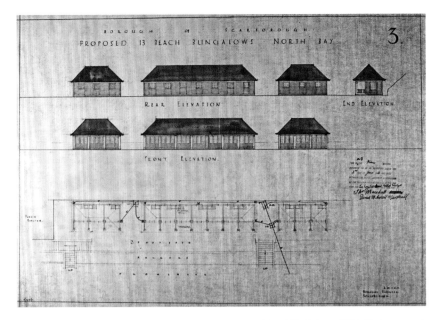

Plans for new municipal huts, North Bay, Scarborough, North Yorkshire, 1931. Each state-of-the-art hut was equipped with an electric grill. These huts were recently demolished as part of the area's coastal regeneration. (The North Yorkshire County Record Office: DC/SCB 3120)

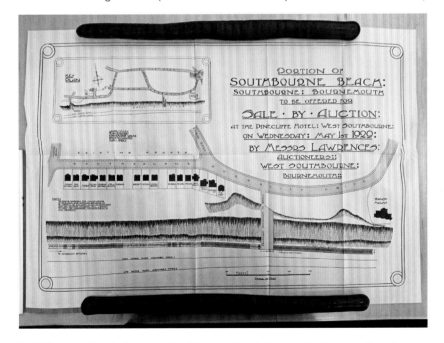

In 1929 several freehold lots at Southbourne Beach, Dorset, for 'the erection of canvas bathing tents, canvas hut or wooden hut or huts in brick, stone or reinforced concrete' were sold by auction. (Hampshire Record Office: 12M86/2/4)

FISHERMEN'S HUTS ON EAST BEACH. HASTINGS.

Fishermen's huts, East Beach, Hastings, Sussex, early twentieth century. The classic timber-framed structure with a pitched roof resembles the beach hut form. Similar huts at Whitstable, Kent, have been converted into holiday accommodation.

nigh on 200 years. Functionally, the beach hut echoes elements of both in that it provides shelter, basic storage, and privacy, although ultimately, of course, the beach hut fulfils a very different purpose. The beach hut today is a simple, informal daytime space, which can be both private and social, a space from which the coast can be enjoyed with the minimum of facilities, a function which has remained basically unchanged since it first emerged.

The architectural form of the beach hut reflects this simplicity; at its most basic, a small, uncomplicated structure is adequate for the requirements of a day at the beach: providing shelter from the elements, refuge from fellow beachgoers, a changing room to slip in and out of swimwear, and storage space for personal items such as towels and reading material as well as stashes of drinks and snacks. Many are equipped with fold-down tables and fittings for bottled gas, and modern huts are usually provided with electricity and even running water.

The popular perception of the beach hut is that of an often brightly coloured, simple, wooden, shed-like structure formed of a single room, usually with gables and a pitched roof. This traditional beach hut form predominates, albeit with variations. Boarding may be vertical or horizontal and can be lapped or tongued and grooved. Gable ends can be decorated or plain, left open, or infilled with trellis, panelling or slatted woodwork. Porticos may have rails or boarded panels and those with windows may have curtains or shutters. Some have verandahs or porches, and doors may be central, or set to the side.

The earliest incarnations of beach huts involved the use of structures already at the shoreline, including the appropriation of abandoned bathing machines and upturned boats, and even railway carriages. The first purpose-built beach huts were wooden, simple, basic and without regulation

Right: Interior of a modern beach hut at Lytham St Annes, Lancashire, displaying good use of space, as well as the luxury of a microwave and extra seating. (Thulborn-Chapman Photography)
Below: Colourful traditional wooden beach huts at Eastbourne, Sussex, with horizontal boarding for the main body and vertical for the doors. (Natalie Schmidt)

The frontages of these prettily decorated huts at Great Yarmouth, Norfolk, are unique to the area. (Richard Bowden)

appeared in all shapes and sizes, often along the top of the beach in a ramshackle fashion. Their easy construction made it a cheap option and, as beach huts were not mass manufactured, smaller companies or individuals were commissioned when required, often from suppliers also in the business of making greenhouses and garden sheds. H. Jones & Sons of 58 London Road, Bexhill, Kent, advertised their 'beach cabin' constructions in the local press alongside their sheds, and W. Seagers of Brightlingsea were builders as well as undertakers.

Did you know?

The oldest public municipal hut has been identified at Undercliff Drive, Bournemouth, 150 metres to the east of Bournemouth Pier. Built in 1909, hut number 2359 was commemorated with a blue plaque from Bournemouth Council in February 2011.

Specifications for beach huts soon became more uniform, dictated by councils for their own stock as well as for privately owned structures. At some resorts where plots were leased from the council, beach hut designs were submitted to the planning department using drawings produced from local builders and carpenters. Plans for huts submitted to the council for sites

These early beach huts at Aldwick Beach, Bognor Regis, Sussex, appear in all shapes and sizes, but were in time replaced with more regular structures.

Municipal beach huts, Bournemouth, *c.* 1909. Hut 2359 with its blue plaque marks it as Britain's oldest identified municipal beach hut. Designed under borough engineer F. P. Dolamore, they have original structural foundations and retain their basic form and character. Simple interiors are painted white and a small wall cupboard provides basic storage. (Thitikorn Wachiraarunwong/ Shutterstock.com)

at Brightlingsea in Essex in the late 1920s were for simple, rectangular, shed-like structures, many informally produced as sketch-plans on headed notepaper or scrap paper.

Canterbury Council stipulations for beach huts at Whitstable and Herne Bay have remained unchanged for decades; those at Whitstable specify that huts should be 10 ft × 10 ft, including 4 ft of covered balcony, and those at Herne Bay are nominally 6 ft × 9.5 ft, including a deck of 2.5 feet. Rather handily, some Herne Bay hut roofs have a forward extension to potentially provide high level storage. Twelve traditional-style wooden beach huts designed for a site at Overstrand in Norfolk in 1969 were also 10 ft square rather than rectangular. All huts under the jurisdiction of Tendring Council are typically constructed of weather boarded timber with pitched asphalt roofs; none of the huts are permitted windows at the sides or rear, and they are to be 'painted within a palette of suggested pastel colours' rather than be treated with wood stain or preserver.

Council-owned beach huts have traditionally been designed in-house by the council architect or surveyor. A simple wooden beach hut design of 1929 with an open front verandah, produced by the council surveyor for a site in Weston-super-Mare, Somerset, had dimensions of 10 ft × 8 ft with a double door and glazed windows opening outwards onto an open verandah.

In subsequent decades the traditional simple beach hut, or variant thereof, has been the most enduring beach hut form, albeit incorporating more durable materials as technology progresses. Today bespoke companies offer features such as 'composite panel technology', modular units and variable roof designs to produce lightweight, maintenance-free huts with long lifespans. In 2014 ten bespoke minimalist huts measuring 14 ft × 11 ft were constructed along the Blackwater Estuary in Essex. They have galvanised box steel frames and concrete composite cladding, and are set on galvanised steel stilts piled 21 ft into the ground. At high tide they are just eight inches above the water so the flooring is slightly domed to allow flood water to drain away.

Terraced beach hut blocks emerged at around the same time as individual huts, becoming current from the early 1900s; they were usually council-built. Among the earliest surviving purpose-built terraced groups are those at Scarborough's South Bay, built 1910/11, and Cromer's Promenade in Norfolk, built in 1912. Terraced beach huts continued to be built throughout the twentieth century, often designed in the architectural style of the time. Notable examples include an attractive 1920s Art Deco brick block at Saltburn and a series of small, utilitarian-style blocks of between nine and twenty brick and concrete huts constructed at various points

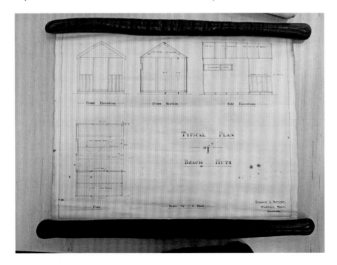

Typical Plan of Beach Huts, n.d. Designed for beach huts to be erected at Farham, Hampshire, this is a fairly standard beach hut design, with the added benefit of a sliding window shutter. (Hampshire Record Office: 64M76/DDS/C20)

An elegant group of huts front Greenhill Gardens, Weymouth, *c.* 1930s. The view is relatively unchanged in comparison with that of today, although the hut gables are currently painted in the seaside pastel palette.

End-of-season beach hut skeletons, near Greenhill Gardens, Weymouth. The same or similar structures appear in the previous image. (Andrew Bone)

Clock café and beach huts, South Bay, Scarborough, built 1910/11. This group was part of a wider scheme to improve visitor facilities and are examples of the first chalet style of terraced beach huts in England. They are Grade II listed. (Steven Barowik)

along the Undercliff at Ovingdean, Saltdean and Rottingdean in East Sussex in the 1960s and 1970s. Chalet-style blocks were popular at many resorts in the 1960s and 1970s, including brick-built sets at Cromer in Norfolk, Bude in Cornwall and Weymouth in Dorset. Some formed large groups, as at Sandbanks in Dorset, and the Solent Beach Complex at Southbourne Beach in Dorset, which contained three blocks of chalet-style beach huts. More recently a terrace of beach huts was built at Worthing in Sussex in 2013 and at Swanage in Dorset.

Beach huts 1–20, Lower Promenade, Saltburn, North Yorkshire, c. 1920. This Art Deco brick-built group is formed of two rows of ten with a central service building and is an exceptional, unaltered structure. They are Grade II listed. (© Lynn Patrick)

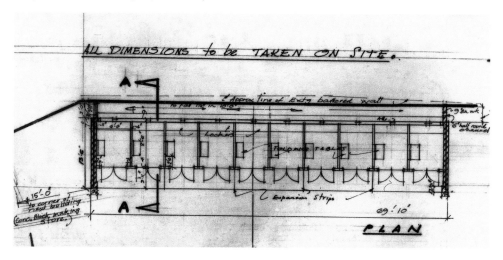

Plan of proposed beach hut block sited at Rottingdean, near Brighton, 1972. The huts were provided with folding tables and lockers, and had outwardly opening doors. (Brighton & Hove City Council DB/D 113/2016/1-4, held at The Keep, Falmer)

Twin lines of beach huts at Swanage, Dorset, appear almost toy-like with their pitched roofs and off-centre, brightly painted doors. Six 'premium' huts are one-and-a-half times larger than standard huts and include a parasol. (Stan Maddams)

The inter-war years were a golden age for seaside architecture as an unprecedented number of people flocked to the nation's seaside resorts; many were adapted and improved to accommodate increased visitor numbers. Civic pride and popular demand led to the introduction of public facilities such as public conveniences, communal shelters and beach huts. Many resorts were transformed in response to a growing obsession with the outdoors, particularly with sunshine and sunbathing. Sun terraces were common and existing or improved promenades allowed for more beach huts to be placed along their lengths. Groups of individual beach huts as well as larger blocks were often incorporated into large-scale complexes. In Somerset, Weston-super-Mare's late 1920s Marine Lake development was built to provide a safe, shallow beach where the tide was always in, and incorporated a Winter Gardens and Pavilion, which opened in 1927, with beach hut structures at one side. This was followed in the 1930s by an Open Air Pool, cinema and airport. At Tinside, Plymouth Hoe, improved swimming facilities were developed from 1913, culminating with an Art Deco lido that opened in 1935.

The use of brick and concrete for beach hut construction was particularly popular in both the pre- and post-war period, including a 1930s block of beach huts at Jubilee Parade, Lowestoft, in Suffolk and a charming line of

The 1930s Art Deco solarium at Branksome Chine, Dorset, was originally flanked by short rows of beach huts.

592. THE NEW SOLARIUM. BRANKSOME CHINE.

In 1988 this attractive set of twenty-one huts to the east of Tinside Lido, Plymouth, were condemned for demolition, but happily they were saved and subsequently restored.

individual brick huts at Hythe in Kent. More unusual styles include groups of tiered beach huts, where individual huts are set into a stepped terrace as at Folkestone in Kent and Tolcarne Beach in Cornwall. Concrete was often used in municipal beach huts of the 1960s and 1970s, especially in chalet designs, and was especially suited to Brutalist designs.

Architect-designed beach huts are increasingly appearing within the landscape, often twisting the traditional beach hut form with jauntily angled roofs as at Hornsea in the East Riding of Yorkshire in 2013 or the innovative 'The Seagull and the Windbreak', built in Boscombe in Dorset in 2011, the country's first purpose-built disabled fully accessible beach huts.

The playful use of design can greatly enhance the basic form of the beach hut. Although many beach huts remain plain and unadorned, often due to council regulations, others are embellished through the use of decorative and shaped gables, finials, gated porches and ornate decorative plaques displaying the name or number of the beach hut.

However, it is colour that remains a major, defining characteristic of the beach hut and, indeed, the use of colour can greatly enhance the aesthetic appeal of even the most basic of structures. The two most popular colour schemes tend to be bold primary colours or a muted pastel seaside palette of pale green, pink, blue and yellow. Primary colours and acid brights can be very dramatic against grassy backgrounds and seascapes, as at Scarborough, Filey and Whitby in Yorkshire, which have undergone bright, even garish colour makeovers in recent years.

Right: This unusual brick-built beach hut at Hythe in Kent is one of a line of huts, all with differently coloured doors. (CBCK/ Shutterstock.com)

Below: The colours of this unusual group of brick beach huts at Folkestone, Kent, add to their unique character. (Eric Young)

Concrete beach huts, Scarborough, North Yorkshire, 1976. These concrete municipal beach huts were very à *la mode*, designed in the Brutalist honeycomb style. (Wrates Photography)

Concrete and steel beach huts, Hornsea, East Riding of Yorkshire, 2003. These huts form part of the renovation of public space along the promenade, which also featured a café, 'wave' lawns and a splash pool. (Jakey Thomas)

Attractive assortment of decorated beach hut gables at Southwold, Suffolk. (Lucy Gleeson, blogger at *Lucy Loves Ya*)

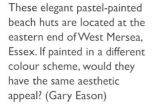

These elegant pastel-painted beach huts are located at the eastern end of West Mersea, Essex. If painted in a different colour scheme, would they have the same aesthetic appeal? (Gary Eason)

This acid-bright colour scheme at Scarborough was applied during a recent regeneration scheme, which saw the renovation and demolition of existing huts and the construction of new sets. (Steve Silver Smith/ Shutterstock.com)

Beach huts at Hove, Sussex, are subject to a designated colour scheme, although doors may be striped or any single colour. Controversy arose in 2011 when a colourful psychedelic pattern was painted; it was not permitted to remain. (Carol Davis)

Local councils often dictate colour schemes, even when beach huts are privately owned. These stipulations can be very strict, as at Hove, where hut roofs and upper sides are painted 'iceplant green' in gloss and the plinth and lower sides in 'dark cherry', although the doors may be painted in either a block colour of the owner's choosing or vertically striped in multiple colours. At Frinton-on-Sea, Essex, beach huts must be painted in approved muted pastel shades, which is written into local legislation as forming part of the promenade's seaside character.

Did you know?

Until the summer of 2016 the beach huts at Appleby, Ryde, in the Isle of Wight were painted a uniform green; however, following a campaign by a local councillor and the majority of owners, a new rule decreed that they may be repainted in any colour ... except for black.

Individuality is permitted at other sites, with the end result often resembling a seashore art gallery. Many huts at Tankerton Slopes, Whitstable, Kent, are painted with individual designs, as are dozens of huts at Viking Bay and Stone Bay, Broadstairs, also in Kent, which contrast with the uniformity of adjacent huts painted in blue and yellow. The line of beach huts along the promenade at Bournemouth leading to Boscombe displays a graded rainbow palette to great visual effect, and elsewhere repeated motifs are used, as at Cromer in Norfolk, where the fronts of some beach huts feature a stylised wave, and an umbrella beneath raindrops and a blazing sun in a knowing tribute to changeable summer weather.

Above: The graded colour scheme of this line of traditional huts running from Bournemouth to Boscombe is visually striking.
Below: Broadstairs beach huts vary widely in their décor and this set contrasts greatly with nearby beach huts sporting regimented blue-and-yellow uniforms. (Jay Garrett)

Personalisation of huts really comes into its own with hut interiors, as there are no restrictions regarding décor. Hut owners decorate their huts in a variety of styles, although vintage and kitsch is enduringly popular. Hut interiors themselves have remained basically unchanged throughout the decades, and are nearly always fitted with simple storage space and a table, often fold-down. The clever use of space and dual-purpose features are increasingly incorporated into designs of new huts.

Hut naming remains the ultimate personalisation, especially for those that are privately owned. Often having seaside and nautical themes, such as *Sea View*, many show a sense of humour through a play on words, such as *Sea-la-vie, Fantasea, Life's a Beach,* and *Seas the Day*, while others encapsulate what their beach hut means to them: *Paradise Found, All Mine, Happy Days, Sioux and Her Tribe,* or the intriguing *Auntie Bong Bong.*

Did you know?

Although beach hut names are common, all beach huts must also have numbers to make them easy to identify. In the words of the Lincolnshire Beach Hut Owners Association, 'Looking for a numbered hut on a promenade is easy; looking for names is a nightmare'.

3
People

It is widely assumed that the hordes of people clamouring to use beach huts of the early twentieth century were 'the toiling classes' and that wider popularity only came following a convalescent stay at the seaside resort of Bognor Regis by George V and Queen Mary c. 1929. Although many 'ordinary' folk did indeed flock to the beaches in their thousands, not all wealthy middle-class families eschewed the seaside and its beach huts, and resorts such as Frinton-on-Sea, which retained their genteel and exclusive characters longer than most, remained popular with the well-heeled middle and upper classes until around the mid-1920s. Frinton's beach huts were popular with families such as Captain Walter Rupert King, his wife Esme and children Denis, Esme Sheila and Thelma; they were a wealthy family of Esher who were regular visitors to the resort in the 1920s. Esme's father was Colonel Frank Robert Simpson, a mining engineer and managing director of the Stella Coal Company, and also a Knight of the Order of St John of Jerusalem, and Esme had grown up at the family mansion, Hedgefield House in Ryton, Blaydon-on-Tyne. She had married Walter in 1919 and their children soon followed; beach trips would often be made by Esme with at least one babe in arms, and the children's nurse to hand.

For most people, however, resorts were not chosen for their social niceties, but for their location and accessibility. Even with improved rail and road transport, people from certain parts of the country tended to visit certain resorts, especially when dependent upon particular rail lines. Londoners have long been regulars to the resorts at the Essex and Kent coasts, while the coasts of Wales and Somerset remain popular with Midlanders. Those nearer the coast were fortunate, with a wider choice of resorts and the option to go more regularly. For those living in Suffolk the resorts of Felixstowe and Lowestoft were attractive, and those in Yorkshire enjoyed resorts such as Filey and Scarborough. Agnes Morgan of Ipswich used a

Esme, Denis and Sheila King and a nurse dressed for afternoon tea at their beach hut at Frinton-on-Sea, Essex, summer 1923. (Reproduced by permission of Durham County Record Office: D/X 1479/17 (15))

hut at Felixstowe while holidaying there in the years following the First World War. Originally from Walworth, she moved to Ipswich, where she married grocer George William Mann in 1915, a widower with four children. The couple ran a popular confectionery shop for many years, and occasional jaunts to the Suffolk coast would have been easy and affordable.

By the 1930s the number of privately owned beach huts being built on both council-owned and private land was increasing, as the attraction of owning a beach hut for breaks away became ever more desirable. Countless wanted and for sale advertisements for beach huts regularly appeared in the local press in this period. Many of those who became owners lived near to their huts and, although many were built by local builders and carpenters, some owners elected to design and build their own. Archie Rand of St Michaels Road in Dovercourt, a director at Bernard's naval outfitters in Harwich, was also a talented carpenter, building the family beach hut in the 1930s in his spare time. He inserted a door at either side, which allowed a choice of entrance depending upon the nature of the east coast winds. The hut could be seen from the family home; this proved an alarming experience during the ferocious storms and floods of 1952, which swept along the south coast and devastated the line of huts. Happily Archie's hut was so robustly built that it survived, although its neighbours were not so fortunate. In the 1960s Winifred, known as Win, and Albert Donnithorne of Bournemouth Park Road in Southend-on-Sea had a nearby beach hut that they used frequently, often accompanied by their close and long-standing friends Patrick and Dorothy Malone and their children.

Not all hut owners lived near to their huts, however. In the 1930s the privately owned Hipkins Beach at East Cliff, Walton-on-the-Naze, leased land known as the Hipkins Estate to several

hut owners. In October 1937 Samuel Lissimore, a grocery van salesman of Collingwood Road, Colchester, had his proposed beach hut approved by the council's planning department and it was built at a site between existing huts *Happy Days* and the unnamed No. 86. Two years later S. E. Barber of north London applied for permission to erect his hut and, although permission was granted by the council on 18 July 1939, enjoyment of his beach hut would have been short lived, if it ever was erected, as war broke out a few months later, and all beaches were closed to the public.

Agnes Morgan, known affectionately as Peg, at her Felixstowe beach hut, *c.* 1919, when she was in her early thirties. (Reproduced by kind permission of Bob Morgan)

Right: Archie and Dora Rand's beach hut at Dovercourt, 1947. Archie Rand, who built the hut, is second from the left and his wife Dora is seated to the right. Their daughter Margaret took the photograph. (Reproduced by kind permission of Gina Stannard)
Below: Win Donnithorne (in the hat) at her beach hut, Southend-on-Sea, with close friends the Malone family, 1968. Win and husband Albert lived at nearby Bournemouth Park Road and used the hut frequently. (Reproduced by kind permission of Chris Scales)

Once the nation's beaches reopened in the later 1940s and 1950s, people once again flocked to the coast. Beach huts that had been dismantled were reassembled by their owners. Improved mobility, growing prosperity, changing social habits and less restrictive leisure time led to a rapid rise in the numbers of people taking seaside holidays, superseding even

Above: Hipkins Beach, Walton-on-the-Naze. Beach huts have been present here for decades. In 2008 some of the older huts were moved to local allotments and replaced by the huts seen to the left of the photograph. (Mary Loosemore)
Left: Agreement for the payment of £2 per annum in compensation for the requisition of a beach hut, 1941. Closed beaches for most of the 1940s prevented beach hut activity, but compensation was available. (Reproduced by permission of the Trustees of the former DLI and Durham County Record Office: D/DLI 7/477/6)

the 1930s. The 1950s and much of the 1960s were the heady heyday of the beach hut, as holiday rentals increased and ownership became ever-more coveted. Waiting lists for beach hut sites grew longer, with impatient would-be owners regularly contacting their local councils to see whether they were any higher on the list. Scores of requests to be added to an increasingly full waiting list for a hut at Hill Head in Hampshire were addressed to Fareham District Council in the 1960s. Some were written on headed business notepaper, including one from a local bank manager who perhaps hoped that his social standing might bolster his request. Another thought that they should be allocated a hut because it would be beneficial to overseas students staying with them in the summer. To address issues of demand *vs* supply, many local authorities began to tighten rules regarding applications and people living outside council jurisdiction were dropped from many waiting lists.

This did not happen simultaneously, nor universally, however, and at some resorts hut sites continued to be leased to people from further afield, often to the consternation of people living in the immediate area. This was perhaps the case in 1950, when dairy farmer Albert Allercot of Bradford-on-Tone in Taunton leased a vacant site on the foreshore at Minehead where he erected a wooden beach hut, *Hillview*, named after his house. Just three years later the lease was sold to local man Mr Cox, who lived in a large detached house in Paganel Road and retained the hut name. Complaints were made to Norfolk's Overstrand Parish Council in 1969 when it was discovered that, of twelve beach hut sites allocated at Overstrand Beach, only two had been allocated to locals and, although five were from elsewhere in Norwich, the rest were from much further afield – from Wisbech, Leicester, Letchworth, Whetstone and Derby. To make matters worse, the owner of Beach Hut No. 2 had violated the terms of his lease by advertising the hut for sale in the local paper, asking for 'offers'.

Not unsurprisingly, the practice of subletting was prevalent and, although not prohibited everywhere, there were strict rules governing hut leases. As early as 1914 two owners of

Beach huts and beach lovers at Hill Head, Dorset. The huts were much coveted in the 1960s, and are the centre of a close-knit hut community today.

Fun at the beach hut, Bexhill-on-Sea, c. 1951. Rupert Watson, son of solicitor Colonel William Watson of Barnard Castle, Durham, spent several summers at Bexhill-on-Sea as a child with his nurse on hand. (Reproduced by permission of Durham County Record Office: D/Wn 28/26)

Scarborough huts were reprimanded by the Borough Council for displaying *To Let* cards in their hut windows. One responded contritely that he had removed the card, but the other transgressor, who had leased her hut for much of the summer to families from Huddersfield and Sheffield, as well as to local families, was less sorry and removed her card 'under as a gentle a protest as I can convey' and went on to say that that, 'The principle of sub-letting as a mutual convenience being allowed, the scarcity of huts acknowledged, is it quite reasonable to deprive us of any official intermediary and then bring us to book for taking the most obvious and direct method of communication with visitors?' In the 1950s the Urban District Council of Frinton and Walton allowed subletting at Frinton only for 'a period of less than seven consecutive days' and restricted it to 'persons residing in the licensee's house or rooms', although for Walton huts this was extended to persons residing within houses or rooms anywhere within the Urban District Council jurisdiction.

When people wished to sell their huts they were often provided with a list of several names from the top of the waiting list. Often this worked smoothly, but sometimes the system was circumvented. In one instance the transfer of a lease to a close friend was permitted because, as was noted, 'she has been sharing the hut with you for some considerable time'. A similar request for the transfer of a lease from a Mr L. Fox of Fareham to his friend Mr E. Lavender of Southampton was initially denied but, when the vendor protested that a quick sale was needed because of the 'credit squeeze' and the inconvenience of contacting people on the waiting list, the council relented and Mr Lavender became the happy owner of Beach Site No. 4, albeit with a doubled site rent as an 'outsider'.

North Bay, Scarborough, c. 1912. The huts in the background were recently built when this image was taken, and were instantly popular. They have recently received a colourful makeover.

THE BATHING HUTS AT THE NORTH SIDE SCARBOROUGH.

In 1934 the sender of this postcard showing Preston Promenade at Paignton in Devon marked the hut they intended to use later in the holiday with a cross.

81168 Preston. The Promenade.

The cost of owning a beach hut could be expensive, with ground rents and rates payable to the council often amounting to a sizeable sum, although this varied according to location. Some enterprising folk applied to have existing structures re-sited in less populist areas, as did Mr W. T. Turner of Egremont, who in 1962 applied to Cumberland County Council to relocate a 6 ft × 11 ft one-roomed timber-clad structure from a railway arch to a piece of wasteland on Caulderton foreshore to use as a 'bathing and rest hut (no overnight accommodation)'. Despite having the consent of the lessee, Leconfield Estate, the application was refused, although curiously there is a hut-like structure at the very same spot today.

Did you know?

In 1947 an enterprising individual made an application to Somerset Rivers Catchment Board to use a disused pillbox at Sand Bay, Weston-super-Mare, as a beach hut. Not only was the application refused, it was decided not to grant permission for any other huts to be erected on the banks or foreshore.

For most people ownership of any type of beach hut was unaffordable, impractical, or impossible, due to living outside of a catchment area. Renting a hut while on holiday was therefore the preferred option for many families in order to enjoy a slice of beach hut life. Daily and weekly rentals could be made through local councils, from concessions, or directly from guest houses and hotels, many of whom owned beach huts or else leased huts from the council for exclusive use by their guests.

Hiring a beach hut was an essential part of the Chorlton family's annual holiday to Bournemouth in the 1950s. Wallace Chorlton was a Shropshire miner and Dorothy a part-time cook, and, as with many workers, holidays were restricted to specific factory and colliery closure weeks – in this case the last week in July and the first week of August. The family holidayed at self-catering accommodation near Alum Chine, renting a hut that they used

Canford Cliffs, early 1970s. In the mid-twentieth century the Poole Hotel and Guest House Association leased beach hut Nos 125–133 at Canford Cliffs promenade from the Borough of Poole for the use of its guests. (© John Hinde Archive)

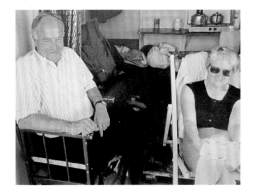

Wallace and Dorothy Chorlton enjoying their beach hut near Alum Chine, Dorset, 1970s. The hut is cosy, with a carpet, table, seating, and, most importantly, a kettle. (Reproduced by kind permission of Ruth Chorlton)

every day, for shelter when the weather turned, and for changing in and out of beach clothes. The children, Susan, Edward, Ruth and Mark, stashed their beach 'tranklements' there, while as teenagers Susan and Edward used it to change for midnight swims with friends and for chatting afterwards. For Wallace and Dorothy the beach hut was perfect for making endless cups of tea, as it had a Calor gas ring as well as a space to prepare lunch.

Company Director Ernest Hutton and his wife Iris with their children Robert and Margaret outside the beach hut they hired while holidaying at Colwell Bay, Isle of Wight, c. 1962. (Reproduced by kind permission of Margaret Buchanan)

The Colwell Bay brick-built beach huts c. 2008, prior to demolition. The huts were rented on a casual weekly basis during the summer season by the local authority and were located next to privately owned beach huts. (Adrian Steel)

Hengistbury Head, Dorset, looking towards Mudeford. A resurgence in the beach hut's popularity in the mid-1990s saw huts here exchanging hands for unprecedented prices. (Ian Duffield/Picfair.com)

Beach huts and beach office, Poole, Dorset, built 1982. This structure is part of a series of similarly designed blocks built from the 1960s onwards. When many resorts were bulldozing their beach huts, in Poole it was business as usual. (Dawn Verdaguer)

Hiring a beach hut was also a major part of the Hutton family holiday in the early 1960s. They travelled from their home in Highgate in North London by train to the Ontario Guest House in the Colwell Bay area of the Isle of Wight. Long and happy days were spent at the beach hut, and evenings at the guest house were enjoyed by the Hutton parents after the children had gone to bed. Friends were made with another family at the guest house, who rented a hut adjacent to the Huttons', which made the holiday so enjoyable that both families repeated the experience the following year, beach hut included.

The 1970s heralded a decline in beach hut use, reaching a low point in the 1980s as British seaside holidays were eschewed in favour of cheap holidays abroad, and the cost of holidaying at the coast in hotels and guest houses became unaffordable to many. Widespread demolition of council beach huts took hold, although a few resorts bucked the trend as at Cromer and Sandbanks, where beach huts continued to be built. Demolition was perhaps premature as, just a short time later, there began a renaissance in popularity, as early as 1986 in some places, which gained momentum in the mid-nineties. Some owners, of course, had never given up on their beach huts, and for other long-term beach users eventually owning a hut was a natural progression.

Pauline and Bert Raby of West End near Southampton were already a valued part of the beach community at Monk's Hill, Lee-on-Solent, where they enjoyed sailing and swimming for many years before obtaining a beach hut there in 1999–2000, allowing more frequent visits with family and friends. They were devastated when on 5 November 2009 their hut was destroyed by an arson attack that also damaged adjacent huts. Bert designed a new, superior hut, which was completed by spring 2010, and it went on to survive the heavy storms and flooding of 2014 intact.

More than just a place in which to change and shake sand from shoes, beach huts are much loved by people that have used them and continue to do so, as social spaces to share with family and friends. Beach hut communities are an important part of beach hut life, and are often places where friendships are forged. Many hut associations have regular social gatherings and rally around when needed. When the Rabys' hut was destroyed, the local Beach Hut Association and other hut owners organised a surprise party for people to bring replacement items. For others the beach hut is a place of calm for relaxation or escape. Speaking in 2005, the former Chairman of the Southwold Beach Hut Owners' Association Dr Slim Dinsdale explained: 'There's something quite unique and magical about sitting in a beach hut on a sunny day ... even when a storm is raging. You just have your own little piece of isolation and escapism and it's absolutely wonderful.'

Pauline and Bert Raby celebrating their wedding anniversary at their beach hut at Lee-on-Solent. The hut has been used for many celebrations and gatherings, both spontaneous and planned. (Reproduced by kind permission of Lorna Chapman)

Solitary beach hut, Cromer, Norfolk, following high tide damage in 2013. Beach huts are very vulnerable to the coastal elements, and their destruction can be devastating to hut owners. (Matt Briston)

Relaxing at the Raby beach hut. (Reproduced by kind permission of Lorna Chapman)

4
Places

The coastline of Britain is peppered with beach huts, but they are by no means evenly spread, being absent in some seaside landscapes and yet dominating others. No comprehensive survey of the nation's beach huts has been carried out, although regional and local reviews have been undertaken by some local authorities as part of regeneration and heritage strategies. The following hut jaunt around the country is brief, and is by no means exhaustive, but provides a glimpse into the variety and location of Britain's beach huts.

The coast of Scotland stretches for over 8,000 miles and contains many expansive sandy beaches, yet beach huts are rare within the landscape. Several resorts, including Brodick on the Isle of Arran, Prestwick's North Beach, and the popular seaside town of Aberdeen, once had full beaches lined with beach huts. There are a just a handful of beach hut sites in Scotland today, most notably the group of forty-four wooden structures at the seaside village of Hopeman on the coast of the Moray Firth. Beach huts have been present here for decades, although they are for the benefit and enjoyment of locals rather than being available to tourists, and are highly sought after, with over fifty people on a ten-year waiting list. In contrast, at nearby Findhorn's North Beach a group of thirty privately owned traditional-style beach huts, spaced far apart long the top of the beach, have not been universally popular due to concerns that they compromise the beach's wild nature. Further south in Berwickshire,

The beach huts at Hopeman are painted in different colours and designs. They are part of a community project and cannot be sold for profit, and thus retain a character that quite literally money cannot buy. (Mike Stephen)

Coldingham Bay has a long tradition of beach huts. Around sixty council-owned huts are leased on a long-term basis, and their scarcity makes them much sought after.

The coastline of Northumberland and Tyne and Wear has over thirty miles of sandy beaches in Northumberland alone and, although there has been a smattering of beach huts here and there over the years, none have endured to form part of the historic landscape. This is in part due to the restriction of coastal recreational use by coalfields and associated industrial and urban development, and commercial ports. Changes are afoot, however, as coastal regeneration schemes take hold. In 2009 a set of twenty distinctive rental huts were built at Blyth's southern beach. Until mid-2016 they could claim to be the only beach huts in Northumberland, but this reign ended with the construction of eight traditional but gaily painted rentable beach huts at Little Shore, Amble, as part of the regeneration of Warkworth Harbour.

The Durham coastline has also been largely devoid of beach huts, as almost half is formed of various developments, working docks and harbours. Recently the Durham Heritage Coast, which runs from Sunderland to Hartlepool, has emerged from its industrial past and may yet follow Northumberland's example with the beach hut construction.

North Yorkshire's coast south of Redcar includes the scenic North York Moors National Park, which has little development. From this point coastal resorts frequently have beach huts in their midst, often where there has been a long tradition. Redcar and Cleveland Borough Council have plans to expand the number of huts at Redcar's Esplanade and Saltburn's Lower Promenade as there is a lengthy waiting list for Saltburn's current twenty. The major harbour towns of Whitby and Scarborough both have brightly coloured beach huts located away from their historic cores. Several popular seaside resorts lie along the East Riding coast. Filey and Bridlington have a host of council-owned traditional and terraced beach huts for hire, the latter at Princess Mary Promenade, North Marine Drive, South Cliff and Belvedere, painted in both seaside pastel and bright colours. Withersnea and Hornsea are not traditional beach hut resorts, although the latter now possesses a modern group of steel and concrete construction built in 2003.

Blyth beach huts in the snow. The huts have a 'green' living roof and are stained with bright colours rather than being painted. Each hut was named by children from the local school. (David Ford)

Brightly coloured traditional beach huts stretch as far as the eye can see along the seafront at Whitby. (Allan Harris)

The coast of Lincolnshire between Mablethorpe and Skegness contains long fine beaches and is the county's main holiday area. The main groups of beach huts are in and around Mablethorpe, including an unusual 1950s concrete and asbestos group between the seafront and Seabourne Road, some classic wooden huts at Sutton-on-Sea, and a colourful line of gaily painted huts along the promenade at Sandilands. A more recent development as part of a replacement hut scheme includes a group of 103 brightly painted and well-equipped beach huts.

'Pagoda' huts, Mablethorpe, rear of Seaholme Road, c. 1953. This unusual but compelling row of huts are built from reinforced concrete, with curved asbestos cement roofing sheets creating a pagodaesque roof. Windows originally flanked metal French doors. (Martin Parratt)

The bright colours and bold forms of the beach huts at Wells-next-the-Sea are all the more striking with their pine tree backdrop. (Richard Bowden)

Beach huts and café, Cromer. This 1930s Art Deco building incorporated beach huts as an integral part of its design and is a significant part of West Promenade. Severely damaged in storms of 2013, it was recently renovated. (Courtesy of North Norfolk District Council)

The Norfolk and Suffolk coasts are characterised by colourful seafront coastlines lined with brightly painted beach huts and many sloping sandy and shingle beaches. A rich and eclectic array of beach huts of all shapes and sizes includes the traditional wooden huts nestled among the sand dunes at Old Hunstanton and individually painted huts set just above the beach at Cromer. The beach at the long-established resort of Wells-next-the-Sea is home to one of the most famous groups of beach huts in Britain.

Great Yarmouth has a long-standing beach hut tradition that today includes privately owned traditional candy-striped huts, which are spaced pleasingly wide apart for privacy, as well as rows of council-owned huts along the promenade. Nearby Gorleston has a similarly long tradition, but in 2011 the last of its huts, a privately owned brick block of twenty-one

The design and colour scheme of these Lowestoft beach huts make a pleasing combination. (Glen Scott)

units on the promenade, was demolished following safety concerns. Immediate demand for their replacement led to moves to construct traditional-style timber huts on the same site. Suffolk's quirky beach huts include groups at Lowestoft and the famous huts at Southwold as well as a set of twelve traditional huts at Sizewell.

Southwold is famous for its colourful and characterful 300-or-so beach huts along the shore. (Pete Tedder)

The Essex coastline is dominated by a string of seaside resorts under the jurisdiction of Tendring Council, who own 3,214 beach hut sites at Clacton-on-Sea, Holland-on-Sea, Walton-on-the-Naze, Frinton-on-Sea, Brightlingsea, Dovercourt and Harwich. Most huts are privately owned and leased from the council. Other Brightlingsea huts are managed by the town council and some at Walton-on-the-Naze are owned by the Walton Pier Company. The extent of the beach huts along this stretch of coast is best appreciated from an aerial view; the huts run along the length of the promenade at Frinton-on-Sea almost continuously to Walton's Southcliffe Promenade, terminating at Walton Pier. Another line leads from the north end of East Terrace to the privately owned group at Hipkins Beach. Along the coast Mersea Island contains an attractive pastel-painted group at West Mersea's Victoria Esplanade, which garners more attention than plainer huts nearby. Colchester Borough Council owns around 384 beach hut sites along the Esplanade between Seaview Avenue and Broomhills Road, which they lease to residents on a long-term basis, and a small group of traditional-style huts for daily hire has been established at Maldon's Promenade Park in the Blackwater Estuary.

The most prominent seaside resort along the Thames Estuary is Southend-on-Sea, although beach huts in this area are concentrated to the east, along Thorpe Esplanade. Further east at East Beach, Shoeburyness, a group of traditional-style beach huts contrasts greatly with a nearby line of modernist huts built in 2013. Across the Estuary lies the Isle of Sheppey in Kent, which, despite having several beaches at Sheerness, Minster Leas, Little Groves and Leysdown-on-Sea, until 2013 had no beach huts. A two-year pilot scheme set up by Swale Council and Minster Beach Hut Association built thirty-five new huts along the Leas, nineteen of which were privately owned.

Kent's coast has several popular seaside resorts, notably Whistable, Herne Bay, Margate, Broadstairs, and Ramsgate, whose beaches are heavily used. All have beach huts, although the group at Margate is located at Westbrook Bay to the west. The main suppliers of beach hut sites in the region include Canterbury City Council, Whitstable Harbour Board and Thanet District Council, the latter with hireable huts at ten bays along the coast. Canterbury City Council manages 650 privately owned beach huts, mostly at Tankerton and West Beach, Herne Bay. The beach huts in this region tend to be traditional in style, although personalisation is notable around Whitstable. Broadstairs possesses a stunning collection of traditional and terrace beach huts, especially at Viking Bay and East Cliff Promenade, and smaller groups of traditional-style huts are located at Louisa Bay and Dumpton.

'Marmite' beach huts, Shoeburyness, 2013. These seven huts divide opinion. Designed to reimagine beach hut typology, they have undulating 'green' roofs and are largely prefabricated from recycled timber pallets, with panels infilled with pebbles, gravel, glass and shells. (Simon Kennedy)

Minster's beach huts are a bigger and bolder version of earlier traditional huts. (Timothy Older, SYMPhotography)

Beach huts at Tankerton Slopes, Whitstable, are renowned for their decorative exteriors. (John Perriam)

Three types of beach hut at Broadstairs: traditional forms and chalet-style, both painted in blue and yellow, with a row of mostly plain traditional huts at their feet. (Jay Garrett)

Further south along the coast at Kingsdown and St Margaret's Bay, Dover District Council leases beach hut sites and, with just twenty-three sites at Kingsdown, there is a long waiting list. The huts here are generally wooden and traditional in style although, without stipulations, they vary somewhat in size and dimensions. The seaside town of Folkestone to the west of Dover has a far larger number of beach huts, and also a wider range of styles. Further south, the renowned Romney Marsh beaches of Dymchurch, Greatstone, St Mary's Bay, Dungeness and Littlestone are generally flat and expansive, each with their own special character, with jaunty groups of brightly coloured beach huts at Dymchurch and Littlestone.

The southern English coast is rich with clusters and lines of beach huts, beginning in East Sussex, which has a long tradition of recreational beach use. There are no beach huts at Camber Sands itself but Rother District Council provides facilities for beach huts in Bexhill, where around twenty temporary sites and 100 permanent beach hut plots are available for licence along East Parade, West Parade and Glyne Gap. The region is dominated by traditional-style wooden beach huts, including those at Bulverhythe and St Leonards West Marina.

Traditionally and brightly painted huts at Eastbourne are located on Grand Parade, Sovereign and Holywell areas, the latter more suited for those who prefer a remoter location. Large and extra-large huts are provided at Holywell and Sovereign, which also have running water and USB charging points. Of the sixty beach huts between Seaford Head and the Martello Tower, just twelve are council-owned and leased to Seaford residents, with an unsurprisingly long waiting list.

Brighton's resort sites of Saltdean, Rottingdean, Ovingdean and Madeira Drive are linked by the long promenade of Undercliff, along which there are occasional small blocks of distinctive mid-twentieth-century brick beach huts leased by Brighton & Hove Council; the waiting list is currently closed. Nearby Hove has a prominent set of relatively recent wooden beach huts that are equally in demand. At Worthing in West Sussex there are currently 131 council-owned beach huts available for hire located between Heene Road and Grand Avenue, as well as some private beach hut sites. Council huts are currently characteristically white with black pitched roofs, although some gables show bright flashes of

Bexhill-on-Sea beach huts in an elegant setting. (Simon Keep)

colour. To discourage sale for profit an owner must apply to the council for a new licence to be issued to a potential buyer, together with a payment of three times the annual licence fee or 10 per cent of the sale price.

Distinctive traditional wooden beach huts groups at both Littlehampton and Bognor Regis are painted in bold colours, with yellow as an accent colour. Those at Littlehampton are set in fourteen curved groups of varying numbers on the beach, and those at Bognor have a grass setting. Beach huts have been present at Bognor's Aldwick Beach since the early twentieth century, and today's huts have shallow pitched roofs and are painted in muted tones. As expected, demand is very high and there is a long waiting list.

As the coast curves westwards, it forms part of an Area of Outstanding Natural Beauty. The resort of West Wittering is known for its long line of 161 mostly privately owned traditional beach huts with overhanging gables and open porches, which form part of the sand dune and beach landscape. Naturally, demand for hut ownership here is high, and a charge is levied for being on the waiting list.

Garage-style beach huts, Saltdean, near Brighton, built c. 1965. These were built as part of a series of brick-built beach huts along Undercliff in the 1960s and 1970s. The original design was for twenty huts, although eighteen were built. (Paul Gillett)

The beach huts of Portland might not be the brightest or showiest, but their special character is bound up with their setting, which is protected by local legislation. (Martin Piccadilly)

The Solent region contains several historic beach hut sites managed by local councils, including a set of 100 attractive pale green, blue and pink beach huts along Southsea seafront managed by Portsmouth City Council. There are also over 700 privately owned beach huts at Barton-on-Sea, Hordle Cliff, Milford-on-Sea and Calshot, curated by New Forest District Council. Regulations for the rental of the unerringly popular beach huts at Gosport and Lee-on-the-Solent are strict and include three-year terms and are for residents only. The face of the seafront at Milford-on-Sea changed forever in February 2014 following the large-scale destruction of many of its iconic concrete beach huts by violent storms. The site was cleared and an innovative replacement seafront incorporates 119 new beach huts that form part of the seafront defence.

Across the Solent on the Isle of Wight there is an historic tradition of beach hut use, which has created a series of close-knit beach hut communities. Beach huts at the resorts of Appley, Puckpool, Dunroamin Beach, Little Stairs, Colwell, Gurnard and East Cowes are privately owned on land leased from the council. Many huts on the Isle of Wight are traditionally painted dark green, including the small group at Esplanade, East Cowes, which are stylistically similar to the earliest municipal huts at Bournemouth; recently there have been moves for other colours to be introduced, as at Appleby, while Dunroamin Beach has many colourful beach huts. As well as council sites, there are also several private beach hut concessions at Sandown, Small Hope Beach, Ventnor and Colwell.

Returning to the mainland, the Dorset coast is characterised by a string of historic beach resorts, many with a long and strong beach hut tradition. There are 158 privately owned huts on Friars Cliff beach, eleven on Gundimore beach and around 150 on Avon Beach. Further west are the iconic resorts of Alum Chine, Durley Chine, Bournemouth, Boscombe and Southbourne. The wonderfully eclectic nature of the hundreds of Dorset beach huts stems from incremental and ad hoc development of beach huts and promenades over decades, ranging from Bournemouth's early municipal huts to the modern seafront developments at Alum Chine and the newly regenerated Overstrand building with its innovative artificial Surf Reef.

Demand for ownership is high in Bournemouth, as around 70 per cent of beach huts are privately owned, the remainder rented out by the council. Poole Council have a larger stock

Canford Cliffs, Dorset, is the perfect setting for these nestling beach huts. (Julie Noble)

of beach huts to lease, but only around sixty-four are for short-term hire, at Sandbanks Shore Road, Canford Cliffs, Branksome Chine and Branksome Dene, and 1,100 are restricted to residents only. Away from the bustle of Bournemouth and Sandbanks areas, a quieter, less intense beach hut experience is enjoyed at the remoter resort of Fishermans Walk, close to the historic Cliff Lift, which allows summer beach access.

Did you know?

The Bournemouth area has over 1,900 huts, equating to around one in ten of the country's beach huts.

The resorts of Studland and Swanage have long-standing beach hut traditions stretching back for over a century. Today there are around 260 huts dotted along the beach at Studland, some at the shoreline, and others further back, secluded among the dunes. Swanage contains a fantastic variety of beach huts, ranging from the plain and uniform to the two tiers of sixty beach huts built in 2014 as part of the Swanage Seafront Stabilisation Scheme.

The stretch of Purbeck Heritage Coast between Swanage and Weymouth is devoid of beach huts, but the huts at Weymouth more than make up for this. The elegant wooden group at Greenhill Gardens, once painted an equally elegant white, now have blue doors with gables painted in seaside pink, green and yellow, slightly at odds with their style. A block of single- and two-storey 1920s chalet-style blocks front Greenhill Esplanade and there is a group of 1960s chalet-style huts at the Greenhill Play Gardens. The beach itself has a series of distinct, cube-shaped, white-painted wooden huts with sloping roofs, not usually seen elsewhere in Britain, although they are stylistically similar to those on Belgian and French beaches.

Although also having a long beach hut tradition, the Isle of Portland is very different in character to its bustling seaside neighbours. The different forms, sizes and orientation of the huts lend a more random character and, as many are sited along field boundaries, they form an intimate landscape together with the low drystone wall and earth bank field boundaries.

These traditional-style wooden Bognor beach huts are bright and bold in yellow, blue and green, and sit well with their grassy surroundings. (Richard Leeming)

These white and bright beach huts of Devon sit well within the landscape. (John McManus)

Porthgwidden Beach Panorama, with beach huts and café in the foreground. (Robert Pittman of Lostwithiel)

Several traditional family seaside resorts lie along the coast towards Devon. The beach at Charmouth has traditional huts alternating in blue and white along the seafront, and brown-and-white huts arranged around a grassy area, which are allocated to residents via a lottery. Lyme Regis has an attractive line of white beach huts with pastel doors on the seafront, which can be hired on a daily, weekly or seasonal basis, and there are several council-owned beach hut sites at Seaton and Beer for seasonal hire, although there is a current waiting list of between five and ten years at Seaton and ten to fifteen years at Beer. For the impatient, four Seaton council beach huts are available for hire on a daily or weekly basis, or there are privately owned huts for short-term rental. Beach huts are expected fixtures at the traditional Devon seaside resorts of Budleigh Salterton, Sidmouth, Exmouth, Dawlish Warren, Teignmouth, Torquay, Paignton and Brixham, and beach huts in this region remain popular.

The rugged Cornish coast contains many fine sandy beaches extensively used for bathing and surfing, yet it is not overly populated with beach huts. Most are sited along the Celtic Sea coast and include the 1950s and 1960s chalet-style beach huts at Porthgwidden near St Ives. Newquay Bay is host to several secluded coves, including those of Lusty Glaze and Tolcarne, both of which have a long history of beach huts set at the head of the beach. Both have terraces of huts; those at Lusty Glaze are white and those at Tolcarne are painted white with primary-coloured fronts. Tolcarne also has more recent traditional wooden beach huts as part of a regeneration programme. A little further north the seaside resorts of Crooklets and Bude have recently undergone a phase of beach hut renewal and replacement, and striking colourful huts continue to be part of the landscape.

Into North Devon, the historic traditional resorts of Westward Ho!, Woolacombe and Ilfracombe are renowned for seaside activity, and there are several beach hut sites, perhaps the most iconic being the privately owned huts at Woolacombe, a jaunty group painted white with boldly painted doors. The coast of Somerset has been largely devoid of beach huts for a long time; the major beach resorts of Minehead, Brean and Burnham-on-Sea have none. The twenty-four traditional-style blue, green and lilac huts at Royal Sands, Weston-Super-Mare, are relatively recent additions, built in 2015. The return of beach huts to Weston's promenade has not been universally popular, not least because they obstruct views and are larger than the planned dimensions. Plans for further huts are currently on hold.

Did you know?

Before the huts were even built, the year-long leases of the beach huts at Weston-super-Mare were controversially sold on a famous online auction site by North Somerset Council in April 2015. Twenty-three people bid on the first lease, which finally sold for £2,650; each of the remaining twenty-three leases were sold every day subsequently.

The Welsh coastline covers some 735 miles, with most development seen on the northeast and southeast coasts. The south coast resorts are popular with day visitors as at Barry, and Langland Bay in the Gower peninsula, both of which have impressive beach huts. The latter is famous for its early 1920s green-and-white beach huts, which line the bay for almost a mile, while the twelve colourful huts lining Barry Island beach are more recent.

The Llŷn Peninsula is notable for having several resorts with distinctive beach huts, including those at the sheltered Llanbedrog Beach, where seventy brightly painted traditional huts occupy the same location as beach tents had done decades earlier. Huts at Abersoch are set along the beach head. North Wales has several traditional seaside holiday resorts,

The elegant and iconic beach huts of Langland Bay stretch for much of its length. (Leighton Collins/Shutterstock.com)

Above: The new private huts at Lytham St Annes. (Stuart Robertson)
Left: These striking beach huts at Barry Island were part of a £3 million regeneration that also incorporated new walkways, toilets and a water feature. Six large and six small huts are available to rent. (Hugh Trainer)

including Rhyl and Llandudno with heavily used beaches especially by day visitors. Rhyl once had beach huts lining the promenades but they have long since been removed, although there are moves towards their reinstatement.

The exposed coastlines of Lancashire and Cheshire extend to nearly 299 miles and contain the resort towns of Blackpool, Cleveleys, Lytham St Annes and Southport. Despite the usual seaside trappings, Blackpool and the neighbouring area of Clevelys were never really beach hut resorts, although in 2014 there were plans for five huts at Blackpool's Waterloo Headland on the Promenade and, after an absence of over twenty-five years, beach huts have made a popular return to Lytham St Annes. To the north the broad and shallow expanse of Morecombe Bay has extensive flats and salt marshes with relatively little recreational development, although the resort of Fleetwood has a lovely row of traditional beach huts, which contrast with a modernist block of ten built on the promenade in 2016.

The final stretch of coast takes in Cumbria, the northernmost county in England. There are no beach huts as such, although there were once randomly sited wooden beach huts at the top of Seascale Beach and possibly also Brayston Beach, which survived until at least the third quarter of the last century.

5
Present

The popularity of the beach hut shows no sign of waning, with both private and municipal beach huts being built to meet demand. The beach hut is now a quintessential part of the seaside and, interestingly, its appeal transcends generations and social groups. Beach huts are just as likely to attract hen parties as they are retired couples and family groups, and, with improved facilities allowing disabled access and the introduction of larger huts, they can now offer an inclusive experience.

While the desirability to own a beach hut might be baffling to some, when beach huts do become available they often sell for huge sums, as gleefully reported each year in the regional and national press. That said, sometimes the term 'beach hut' is used loosely and includes chalets with sleeping accommodation. Nevertheless, in 2016 a plain, no-frills, traditional beach hut on Abersoch's beach front sold for an unprecedented £153,000, greatly exceeding the guide price of £91,000; however, more modest sums are usually reached, as at Mersea's Victoria Esplanade where a hut recently sold for £28,000.

For those unable to buy, whether through availability or affordability, beach hut rentals remain extremely popular, both of council stock and also privately owned huts. Flexibility of rentals in many areas means that huts may be rented daily, weekly, monthly, seasonally, annually and sometimes even in winter. The demand for rentals can be overwhelming at some resorts. In 2014, when the waiting list for beach huts at Sandbanks in Dorset opened for the first time in seven years, an estimated 3,500 people tried to apply online, causing Poole Council's website to crash under the strain. To tackle demand, many councils have recently rethought their leasing policies, replacing indefinite renting with fixed leases and closing waiting lists, as well as planning more huts to be built.

Did you know?

Despite there being over 1,100 beach huts within Poole's Council stock, the demand for them is so high that estimated waiting list times range from eleven years for a hut at Sandbanks to nineteen years at Canford Cliffs.

The desire for the beach hut experience clearly remains attractive. The value of the beach hut is more than monetary. Whether enjoyed by a group of friends cooking sausages in a Birchington beach hut on a cold Christmas morning, or by families celebrating golden wedding anniversaries, the beach hut is often a place of shared experiences. It is regarded with affection and familiarity and, although huts can be chic and modern, it is often the nostalgic, quaint and kitsch image that prevails.

The beach hut has pervaded the arena of popular culture in various guises. 'The Beach Hut' is a popular name for beachside cafes and bars, as well as being used as a theme for décor,

The beach hut motif is used here as part of the *Snowdogs by the Sea* installation on Hove Promenade in 2016. This is *Pebbles*, designed by Joanna Martin. (Carol Davis)

The Beach Houses of Margate next to beach huts. The eleven open-plan beach fronted homes were inspired by the architectural form of the beach hut, notably in their proportions and pitched roofs. (Pamela Fray)

with beach hut booths and even whole beach huts being used as outdoor seating areas. Beach huts have supplied the setting for novels and films, and the form of the beach hut is an instantly recognisable and popular motif used to great effect in interior design and various household knick-knacks. There are fabrics and fridge magnets, and even mini DIY flat-pack cardboard beach huts that can be painted.

The beach hut has proved to be the perfect subject for many photographers and artists, and has inspired a string of art projects, among them Tracey Emin's installation of 2000, *The Last Thing I Said To You Is Don't Leave Me Here,* which comprised her blue weathered Whitstable beach hut alongside two photographs of Emin.

The beach hut's representation within the public art arena is a relatively recent and captivating phenomenon. The Folkestone Triennial, an arts charity dedicated to enabling the regeneration of Folkestone in Suffolk through creative activity, commissioned two pieces of beach hut-inspired public art in 2008 and 2012. Richard Wilson's *18 Holes* comprised three 'crazy' brutalist beach huts, each formed from six concrete measured slabs from the former eighteen-hole crazy golf course at the rear of the esplanade. *Beach Hut in the Style of Nicholas Hawksmoor* is a ten-metre tall steel frame structure clad in marine ply, the creation of Pablo Bronstein. It represented a lighthouse as if designed by Hawksmoor, which stood among Folkestone's brightly coloured beachfront beach huts creating 'a sense of folly'.

A Worthing 'folly' was constructed on the beach in 2015 by an architectural firm as a promotional and community engagement project. A temporary timber-framed mirror-clad structure inspired by the traditional beach hut, with gabled structure and Worthing beach hut specifications, camouflaged with its surroundings, much to the bemusement and amusement of the local inhabitants. The allying of art and architecture was also used at the Southbank Centre's celebration of the 1951 Festival of Britain in 2011. Among the architectural projects fourteen custom-built beach huts, which lined the South Bank, were designed by specially invited guests including comedian Phill Jupitus, and artists Grenville Davey and Tim Hunkin.

On a larger and more permanent scale, art and architecture has been successfully deployed as part of several coastal redevelopment schemes. In the mid-to-late 1990s East Riding Council

The renowned installation *18 Holes* by Richard Wilson, Felixstowe. (Richard Gottfried https://hamandeggerfiles.blogspot.co.uk)

commissioned collaborative multidisciplinary teams of architects and artists to devise a regeneration scheme at Bridlington's South Promenade to address the problems of the resort's decline as a holiday destination and the desire to renovate the promenade by 'building in humour and fun', using quality design and materials. The setting and views of the beach huts are a significant part of this design, and occupy a semi-public space. Importantly, tourism was estimated to have subsequently increased by at least 20 per cent in the first year alone.

The successful incorporation of beach huts into designs that benefit the wider community is proving popular. Beach huts at Milford-on-Sea were incorporated into a £1.2 million coastal flood defence scheme commissioned by the New Forest District Council, completed in 2017. Designed by a team of architects and engineers, a row of 119 brightly coloured beach huts are set into the sea wall below an elevated promenade, effectively becoming part of the architectural infrastructure.

At Eastbourne in 2016 an architectural competition was held for the design of four 'bold and imaginative' beach huts to form part of a new cycle route connecting Eastbourne's Towner Art Gallery with the De La Warr Pavilion in Bexhill and the Jerwood Gallery in Hastings. A second competition to design a fifth hut was opened to members of the local community.

Alongside architectural and aesthetic innovations, many local authorities are also recognising the historic value of beach huts as integral elements of a resort. Strict planning regulations at Portland regulate the erection of new beach hut sites on undeveloped and existing sites to preserve the special historic and diverse character of the beach hut: 'it is important that beach huts retain the appearance of temporary timber built structures without permanent foundations in order to preserve their essential character.' The appearance of Frinton-on-Sea's beach huts is also strictly controlled by local legislation, as they are regarded as the 'most characteristic feature of the promenade'. A scheme near Littlehampton in Sussex to reinstate an historic line of beach huts along a stretch of coastal path reinforces this emphasis on historic value. The design is a contemporary twist on the classic beach hut form, with a porch and doors with shutters, although, intriguingly, a triangular roof.

Even where council-owned beach hut stock has been allowed to fall into disrepair, as befell the 1930s beach hut block of fifty-or-so beach huts at Jubilee Parade, Lowestoft, which were closed and sealed off in 2016 due to safety concerns, their long-term future is now a serious consideration, as they form an essential component within the local environment. Temporary

The remodelled South Promenade, Bridlington, with beach huts. (Martin Peters)

beach huts have been installed while the council make a decision on the long-term future of the original block. Programmes to enhance existing coastal assets are increasingly being initiated. New, colourful beach huts have been erected as part of several regeneration schemes of repair and replacement to boost images as traditional family seaside resorts, as at Crooklets and Summerleaze in Bude, Cornwall, and Whitmore Bay, Barry Island in Wales in 2014.

Generally overlooked within the realm of seaside architecture until relatively recently, the beach hut has in recent years been included within publications, talks and events, and is now accepted as forming part of a wider architectural and social history. It has been the subject of academic research, including a doctoral thesis on the beach hut in East Anglia published in 2011, while a collaborative research project between the Courtauld Institute of Art and Birkbeck College in London concerns the history and development of the single room, including the beach hut, for individual use as an architectural phenomenon. The awarding of statutory Grade II listed status to beach huts at Cromer, Scarborough, Saltburn and Weymouth earlier this century provides further recognition of the beach hut as an important architectural and historic structure, and it may be well be that beach huts constructed today may receive similar recognition in the future.

Today the beach hut is an accepted part of the seaside leisure tradition. Groups of huts bring vibrancy and rejuvenation to seaside resorts, and they can help to develop a sense of place and community in an area. They are part of the nation's ongoing social and architectural history; the incorporation of beach huts in seafront regeneration schemes, the installation of new beach huts to replace old and the scores of new beach hut schemes in new locations to meet ongoing demand is testament to their enduring appeal.

Beach huts at Summerleaze Beach. The huts were built to a design chosen after consultation with existing hut tenants and the public, and included extra-large beach huts with disabled access and capacity to seat over twenty people. (John Fielding)

6
What Now?

A piqued interest in beach huts and their wider context can readily be explored further; there are several books dedicated to them, as well as architectural and social history books on the wider British seaside. For the real enthusiast, there is no substitute for hiring or buying a hut, and you might very well like to try before you buy. If so, there are many resorts with different characters to choose from, from bustling Bournemouth to peaceful Portland.

Further Reading

Brodie, Allan, Sargent, Andrew, and Winter, Gary, *Seaside Holidays in the Past* (English Heritage, 2005). *An absorbing collection of photographs from the Historic England Archive capturing the spirit of the English seaside holiday.*

Ferry, Kathryn, *Beach Huts and Bathing Machines* (Shire Publications Ltd, 2009). *An informative and succinct account of the history and development of bathing machines and beach huts.*

Ferry, Kathryn, *Sheds on the Seashore* (Indepenpress Publishing Ltd, 2009). *An illuminating narrative on the history of the bathing machine and beach hut up to the 1970s, interspersed with a travelogue recounting the author's visits to beach huts.*

Field-Lewis, Jane, *My Cool Shed: An Inspirational Guide to Stylish Hideaways* (Pavilion Books, 2012). *Celebrates the humble shed as a getaway and personal space in various forms, and ways to style them.*

Gray, Fred, *Designing the Seaside* (Reaktion Books, 2009, 2nd ed.). *An excellently thorough history of seaside architecture from the eighteenth century to the present day*

Green, Rod, *Beach Huts* (Cassell Illustrated, 2006). *A quirky illustrated celebration of beach huts all over the world.*

Prowse, Angie, *Beach Huts Along the Saxon Shore Way* (Blurb Books, 2009). *An affectionate photographic portrait of people who own the unique beach huts along the North Kent coast, along the old Saxon Shore Way.*

Simpson, Eric, *Wish You Were Still Here: The Scottish Seaside Holiday* (Amberley Publishing, 2013). *An interesting account of how people enjoyed seaside holidays, including how they travelled and where they stayed.*

Williams, Peter, *The English Seaside* (English Heritage, 2013, 2nd ed.). *An enjoyable and affectionate look at all types of English seaside, from fishing villages to resort towns.*

Places to visit

There are many groups of beach huts worth visiting, too many to individually list. However, the famous traditional huts at Southwold are a must, as are the various groups in and around Bournemouth, Cromer and Broadstairs for their variety and historical interest. The Grade II listed beach huts at Cromer, Saltburn, Weymouth and Scarborough are also worth visiting for their historical value. For more modern designs, the structures at Shoeburyness, Hornsea and Mablethorpe are worth seeing, as well as the beach-hut inspired houses at Margate, Kent.

Bournemouth area, Dorset: Up to seven miles of coast contains beach huts, which are concentrated at Alum Chine, Durley Chine, Bournemouth, Boscombe, Southbourne and Fishermans Walk.

Cromer, Norfolk: Cromer seafront has an array of beach huts, including brick-built huts on its East and West beaches and the recently restored 1930s Art Deco pavilion. There are wooden beach huts at nearby Sheringham and Mundesley.

Shoeburyness, Essex: The controversial beach huts are located on East Beach, off Rampart Terrace.

Southwold, Suffolk: The huts line the shoreline from Ferry Road, past the lighthouse and beyond the pier.

Wells-next-the-Sea, Norfolk: The beach is a five-minute drive or half-an-hour walk along Beach Road from the town of Wells. There is a car park and café once you get there though. The beach huts back on to a wooded area and part the Norfolk Coast Path.

Get involved

Associations are a good way to connect with fellow beach hut owners and communities. A National Association of Beach Hut Owners was set up in 2007, but is no longer current. There are a plethora of local associations and, although the following list is by no means exhaustive, it includes the most active:

> Bournemouth Beach Hut Association. www.bournemouthbeachhuts.org.uk
> Clacton and Holland Beach Hut Association www.clactonbeachhut.org.uk
> Felixstowe Beach Hut and Chalet Association www.felixstowehutschalets.co.uk
> Herne Bay Beach Hut Owners Association www.hernebaybeachhuts.com/history.html
> Beach Hut Owners Association Lincolnshire community.lincolnshire.gov.uk/bhoa
> The New Forest Beach Hut Owners Association www.newforestbeachhuts.com
> Poole Beach Hut Tenants poolebeachhuts.co.uk
> Southend Beach Hut Owners Association www.sbhoa.org.uk
> Southwold Beach Hut Owners Association www.southwoldhuts.co.uk
> Tankerton Bay Beach Hut Owners Association www.tankertonbeachhuts.co.uk
> Beach Hut Owners of Walton www.facebook.com/WaltonBeachHutAssociation

For proud beach hut owners, an annual Beach Huts of the Year competition is open to all UK beach huts. Details can be found at www.towergateinsurance.co.uk/home-and-property-insurance/beach-hut-of-the-year.

For the creative, the annual Bathing Beauties Festival, held at Mablethorpe promenade, Lincolnshire, features a competition to design a beach hut: www.bathingbeautiesfestival.org.

For more general seaside heritage-related activity, the Seaside Heritage Network provides membership to professionals working with seaside collections and all those interested in seaside history, heritage and culture. Its aims include the promotion of the value of seaside heritage and culture and to share knowledge and expertise: www.scarboroughmuseumstrust.com/seaside-heritage-network.

Web Resources

If the idea of owning a beach hut appeals to you, check the local press for private sale advertisements, as well as contacting estate agents in the area you would like to buy; beach hut sales particulars often appear on estate agents' websites. If hiring a beach hut appeals, whether for a day, a week or longer, then there are two main options. Privately owned beach huts are regularly listed for hire on www.beachhuts4hire.co.uk and are searchable by resort; beach huts are also advertised for sale here. Information on hiring a municipal beach hut can be found on local authority websites. There are too many to list, but these include:

Canterbury www.canterbury.gov.uk/leisure-countryside/foreshore-services/beach-huts
Christchurch, Dorset Council www.dorsetforyou.gov.uk/article/409581
New Forest: www.newforest.gov.uk/beachhuts
South End: www.southend.gov.uk/info/200307/beaches/87/beach_huts
Tendring: www.tendringdc.gov.uk/leisure/seafront-and-beaches/beach-huts

For the beach hut owner, the Love Your Huts website offers a specialist insurance and risk management consultancy for beach huts, chalets and shepherd's huts. It includes a friendly and useful news section with hints and tips, and there are links to potentially useful associations. www.loveyourhut.co.uk